NOTES FROM A STRANGER
(Extract of life-I)

Na. Ulaganathan

Chennai • Bangalore

CLEVER FOX PUBLISHING
Chennai, India

Published by CLEVER FOX PUBLISHING 2023
Copyright © Na. Ulaganathan 2023

All Rights Reserved.
ISBN: 978-93-56484-38-2

This book has been published with all reasonable efforts taken to make the material error-free after the consent of the author. No part of this book shall be used, reproduced in any manner whatsoever without written permission from the author, except in the case of brief quotations embodied in critical articles and reviews.

The Author of this book is solely responsible and liable for its content including but not limited to the views, representations, descriptions, statements, information, opinions and references ["Content"]. The Content of this book shall not constitute or be construed or deemed to reflect the opinion or expression of the Publisher or Editor. Neither the Publisher nor Editor endorse or approve the Content of this book or guarantee the reliability, accuracy or completeness of the Content published herein and do not make any representations or warranties of any kind, express or implied, including but not limited to the implied warranties of merchantability, fitness for a particular purpose. The Publisher and Editor shall not be liable whatsoever for any errors, omissions, whether such errors or omissions result from negligence, accident, or any other cause or claims for loss or damages of any kind, including without limitation, indirect or consequential loss or damage arising out of use, inability to use, or about the reliability, accuracy or sufficiency of the information contained in this book.

What do you want?

I am getting old. I am going to die.

I want to show this world something.

Something means?

I wanted to write a lot in my youth—novels and modern poetry.

I didn't have money to write and publish. So, I started earning busily and ran towards the same until yesterday.

I don't want to be like that for days and days to come.

So?

I want to see the truth; I want to make it into a book and it should reach everyone.

No... No... Money is the only thing that gets everyone.

Everything else goes to smaller groups.

The world has shaped you wrongly.

So?

Everyone is different in this world.

Everyone lives according to their respective living groups.

He understands what the group conveys to him.

That's right too.

That's right!

People in the world do not need to be the same!

Time varies.

Food is different.

Living space varies.

Dress varies accordingly.

So, what is common to all?

What is the general truth?

He is "life."

His money has to protect that life.

If you can say something common to life money, it will reach everyone.

Are you saying that living beings all have similarities when they are born?

No! No!

The common quality of living things is one.

But it also has great qualities.

So?

The first is general characters, understand?

For all beings have the perception (inborn knowledge), desire, and action.

Special qualities are experiences containing Anavam (ego or sense of self), Kanmam (experience), and Mayai (existence of birth, sustain, and disappearance—the raw material for anything).

To make you understand further it is self-respect (self-esteem/Agangaram) and independence.

What appears, sustains, and perishes is called mayai (in Tamil).

Oh, very good!

Can change human experience.

Self-esteem cannot be replaced by his independence.

Whenever there is an attempted threat to self-independence, there is violence everywhere.

It is the cause of all the world wars, family feuds, etc.

So, what about illusion (mayai)?

Illusion is an important ingredient.

Everything is changing in this world.

Only when one object appears, ceases, and collapses can another appear.

That's right. That's right.

Are you saying the right thing?

What the world has in common is "money" and "self-esteem" (Agangaram).

How can I say this to fix common to all humans?

Yes, you can't.

But understand one fact.

No living being can escape from the cycle of birth, life, and death.

Production of any inanimate object, production of the object, the existence of life of that object and material obsolescence;

nothing is getting out of the cycle of…

Ohhh…

Anyone with the five senses uses them as tools for his life, and the mind, intellect, ego, and Sitham (memory tank).

By organizing these instruments, the special characteristics of living beings are self-esteem (Anavam), experience (Kanmam), and delusion (mayai)

The experience of "Kanmam" can be transformed into, i.e., added to, or reduced to the illusory material attachment and attachment to beings.

But...

But what?

Life is showing its existence through Agangaram which is simply self-respect—independency.

Only by enriching self-respect, self-independence, and the energy battery of self-esteem, can humanity's conflicts be reduced.

So, what happened to his country, group, and money; what's the matter?

Money cannot be generalized; it is related to one's ego (Anavam), experience (Kanmam) and vanity (Mayai).

So, I understand what you say:

abundant wealth, self-independence of the individual's "life," (the regulated ego) and the enrichments of those above two points are important.

This will be the starting point for the journey towards peace and a higher standard of life.

Okay, okay. I'm sleepy. I'm going to bed.

Okay!

Stay wide awake and sleep.

Watch where "I am" in sleep.

In the city of Jacksonville in the state of Florida in the United States of America, the young snow wind blew before the days of Christmas passed, the young heat of the morning sun in the cold, a calm venue.

On the side road, under a broad tree, in a gentle environment, he came.

How did you sleep?

I do not know!

Don't know? No. No. Not noticed?

Didn't notice…

Breathing exercises help observe life.

Ohhh…

There are learned gurus and teachers for that.

Ohhh…

Proper eating habits and breathing exercises on an empty stomach make all the glands in the body work properly.

So…

Only if we get used to bringing the breath under our control, we can understand the nature of our life.

So, a few minutes before falling asleep, air from the abdomen passes through…

Exit through the mouth.

Oh…

We can see that all the system tools in the body slowly stop and because of the stopping, life slowly moves towards the lower abdomen.

Like that.

How do you say it clearly?

Those senses alert in the waking state are now entering an inert state—the sense of touch, sense of taste, ability to see, ability to smell, and ability to listen.

Yes, even though the element has the power to operate properly, the connection to the live battery is cut off.

So, the brain needs to rest.

So, it closes all the sensory doors.

Ohhh.

What will life do?

This is a great question!

It is known that life is releasing itself slightly from the physical field.

Oh…

But, I've read that it blends with cosmic energy.

So, what drives life?

Cosmic power!

Who said so?

Our ancestors.

He sat up straight to listen curiously.

It's a subtle thing,

like jaggery in the mouth of a dumb…

So?

Looks like!

Understood!

But I can't prove it. Has anyone proved it yet?

I do not know.

I am slowly getting into the safety zone!

He doesn't seem to let go.

Where did life come from?

How does it work?

Who runs it?

I have become more alert.

Don't know!

I will tell you from what I read how it works.

If it works like that, then your third question is the answer.

Who directs life?

Nothing appears automatically in this universe!

"Of those objects present only raises…!"

So...

What is not present does not appear.

I don't understand.

Like a mushroom that sprouts the day after it rains.

As of Insect worm species sprouts.

Mushroom seeds and maggot eggs must have been there but we have not noticed them.

And so, it must have the power to drive life!

It could be a cosmic force.

So, all living things do not work in the same way.

Yes...

It's not like that!

Yes...

So, even though life is driven by cosmic power, every living being has different desires.

Where did this desire come to life?

Everything is like this cell phone signal where audio and video come in the air but our eyes don't see it.

But the machine knows!

Yes.

But the power that drives life may be a much more subtle ray movement.

Understood, understood.

Subtle "Sukshuma Shakti" is running this world and universe.

We all worship Him as Lord.

Yes, yes.

Now, our subject is why different desires for each living being.

Those desires are in life.

Yes, there is no need to prove that there are different desires.

But how they operate in life is less clear. The environment in which man is born and the environment in which he grows up are not in the hands of that life.

Yes.

Then, what causes a child to be born to those parents?

In the environment of birth and development, what is seen by the eyes, heard by the ears, tasted, smelled, and felt by the body, are all imprinted in the brain as images. In fact, even words are imprinted as forms of images—pictures!

Ooh!

Why research this? Strictly speaking, the birth of that child to those parents is based on a material system-centered.

That is the only way to experience the pleasures and pains of "Kanmam" (experience).

That's right.

Depending on which area you come from, your habits, character, and interests can be predicted to some extent.

That's right.

So, can you say whether he is good or bad?

There are good people and bad people in every environment and in children who grow up. But this human civilized system exists in an environment where that class discrimination has to happen!

If it is true that the nature of land varies in different parts of the earth, then it is true that the nature of humans and animals living there also differs.

Who decided that you should be born in this particular town in this place at this time?

I'm not really...

Okay, okay.

But here, a living being has to believe in a cosmic power greater than itself!

Desires vary depending upon the environment in which he lives.

The seed of desire depends on the record of his life.

Who instilled desires in life?

I don't know where life is.

Where it is embedded, is a more complicated matter.

Desires came alive.

It is the nature of life.

If there are no desires, there is no life.

That is why some sages and philosophers consider "asceticism" as the supreme state of life.

That's right.

Can desire be eradicated?

Why eliminate it?

"Desire is the cause of action!"

Perception contains the seed of desire.

Life without desire does not take birth!

Desire itself cannot be satisfied.

We see millions of examples.

Desires grow rapidly to enjoy and enjoy…

Taking a new shape…

Pornography is the endless evolution of desire for sex!

How many evolutions of lust drag life to an endless distance?

We have to control.

Strictly speaking, this control itself requires a lot of faith!

That faith will be the leader, the power to guide the desire of man.

That is "virtue" (Aram in Tamil), discipline, and "dharma."

So, is a society with virtue and dharma a peaceful society?

Of course!

It is a peaceful society.

But even there the economic condition is a driving battery for virtue and dharma.

How do you say?

If I want to feed the animals around me and remove hunger…

I need more food. The one who has more food is great in virtue. If I can feed two stray dogs, then there is another one that exists to feed a thousand people.

Here, material wealth determines virtue and dharma!

Therefore, virtue and dharma differ depending on the economic environment.

Depending on it, the nature of adjusting the desire also differs.

It's not going to be very deep.

Oh yes.

The vehicular noise subsided. I strolled in the cool air in the thin shade. There was no sound except for the rustling of leaves.

On the grass in front of a factory, its billboard was embedded with a cement block. I sat on top of it a little. A big truck was coming in the distance.

What is virtue?

What is Dharma?

Yes, yes.

Virtue is the moral code that a person imposes on himself.

Let's look at it this way. For example, a seller of baby milk does not mix cow's milk with any other milk or water.

Selling milk to another person, even if the milk is mixed with water is the virtue that he has determined for himself based on the experiences he has encountered in his life.

It draws a line of control for him.

What is Dharma?

Mm... Mm...

So, dharma is the moral code that a "society" imposes on itself.

If a town decides to sell paddy seeds at the price of ordinary paddy, it is the Dharma of the paddy farmer in that town.

Virtue and dharma control the level of desires.

Its highest level is the highest human civilization.

But the erosion of economic need makes man deviate from virtue and dharma.

If a society that has adopted only virtue and dharma has created a large economic gap among the people of that society, then surely virtue and dharma will be violated.

This is due to the intense nature of desire.

As such, asceticism depends on that social context.

Self-freedom of ego is an inbuilt battery of knowledge, thought, and attitude to this world;

these differ from group to group.

This difference directly affects the economy and labor.

The price of labor for a person depends on the intensity of his desire for labor seller.

Not only that but if the buyer of labor does not know the labor market, the labor provider sells his labor at a good price!

That's right.

And the reverse applies to this one, as well because of the intensity of desire the laborer has to sell his labor even at a very low price.

For example, a mason's hand assistant is a drunkard. If he is physically ill, he will not be able to get a good price for his labor. The master who quotes the price for him…

He will not even give him half of the money even though he got the market rate money.

The reason is that the ill, drunkard worker is not employed by any mason.

Who is responsible for managing his cost of labor?

A solid, good worker who works for the same salary earns more. So, people in that group don't care about virtue, dharma, etc.

There is a middleman called Mestri who speaks a different virtue.

He says that he is giving him a job out of a "dharma thought" and otherwise he would starve.

Well, the sickly, drunken, senile, wage laborer whose physical damage caused by his desire leads him to economic backwardness.

(If in India in my town, we can go to the tea shop next door and drink tea.)

Okay, okay. I got up and started walking saying, "Let's go home and drink tea."

What I would like to say is that the ideal society is one in which both economic prosperity and individual human freedom (ego) are the components of a high civilization.

I am the best, wisest, most skilled, strongest, wildest, with morals and whatever else he says, it is his ego or individual human freedom.

He imagines himself to be what he believes, and his will impress upon him. It is here that his sense organs and the electricity of desire through life drive him to operate.

Today, my mind is very light. I came for a walk and sat under a tree.

Nothing wrong and unnecessary is created in this world! Everything is created for the good! Everything is reciprocal. The truth is that the great power of the universe is cosmic energy. That power did not create life!

Life has been co-existing with cosmic power for ages!

The cosmic power is doing the great technical work of implanting the effects (cause and effect of deeds) as seeds in the brain, in the memory tank called "Sitham."

That act-result, embedded in knowledge, transforms it into the power of the seed of desire, and then into action.

The records of the great things in the environment of human existence are only on the surface of information-based knowledge.

Perception makes decisions motivated by desire. That decision determines happiness and misery, the "life" one deserves to experience.

Is there a life without suffering? Of course not! Ignorance is the cause of suffering.

It can also be said that there is a lack of information. The memory tank known as Sitham is the supreme place of beings. It is like a hard disk of a computer that does not have any traces of previous birth memory but it is embedded with the resultant effects of sin or good deeds to which the present birth is taken place.

The cosmic power—completely empties the traces of the previous life and makes it a tool for the present life, in what socioeconomic environment, in what gender, in what color, height, shape, beauty, structure, birth—makes that life enjoy the fruit of the previous birth in this birth.

Do you believe in pre-birth?

Have to believe.

Unless all human beings have the same genes, there must have been an antecedent.

If thumb impressions and hand lines are unique, so is the experiential record of the antecedent.

It's true.

Beautiful white geese are swimming beautifully in the nearby lake.

All the trees spread their shade on one side.

In the other half, the sunlight was also embedded in the lake.

The place of darkness is actually where there is light! As soon as there is light in the darkness, the darkness disappears and the light fills it, and it does not need any other place!

Ignorance and knowledge are at the same place till we don't know knowledge believes in darkness.

Capital is the "ignorance" of business demand. A man who revolves in ignorance loses his object and suffers.

He worships the cosmic power as a deity to remove ignorance and therefore, he always sees the Lord as a material giver.

He worships.

Indeed, to praise God, to give thanks.

Soft waves of water swayed the shadows like the wind on silk.

Nothing seems so great as the true need of man. However, desires are always springing up from the human mind.

From youth to old age, one's desires are food, lust, and irresponsibility. They are highly introverted and biased. Desire protects those who are fit for providing above those things.

The eyes squinted from time to time. Although there was sunshine, it was not so visible in the thin, warm snow.

Literature emphasizing virtue and dharma lives long.

Literature, music, and dramas are stimuli for emotions to inculcate ethics and Dharmas.

These feelings are always preserved as seeds in the memory of the so-called Sitham.

There is no need for prevailing "truth" between the "creator of literature" and "literature."

That is why literature, however high it may be, cannot be used to establish a new evolution of life.

If that were the case, "Thirukkural" alone would be the supreme literature of this world. It should also have been the scripture of the people of the world.

Everyone wants to live how he wants; he does not want to live by the principles and rules of dharma. So, two things should be discussed here.

A man who lives according to desire.

A defined limit to desire.

Unfettered desires undermine the civility of society. A very simple example of this is that male and female desire, lust.

A higher standard of civilization is:

A man's economic freedom, to get what he wants when he wants it, and to give man the freedom of ego—the instrument that preserves the freedom of life—to it.

Only a government that can be the leader of groups can do these things. A government that does not recognize these two liberties can only propagate a low civilization among its people.

The seeds of antecedent action-result-beneficial desire embedded in the will.

Explain to me properly. I don't understand.

It is the hen that incubates the duck's eggs, even though it is breeding, the hen thinks that everything is her chick. One day, when she goes to the edge of the pond, only the duckling runs away and falls into the pond to swim. The reason is that the knowledge touches the perception (Sitham) and the egoistic feeling that touches the duckling's inborn memory.

Go there and do the "act" of swimming.

I understand now.

Okay, morality and morals differ from age to age. Any vine that grows on its own will only grow haphazardly. It needs a supportive stem to grow upward.

Aram (Aram in Tamil means discipline or virtue) and Dharmam are needed as supplementary aids. This too should be legislated by the leadership of the group's government.

Now, a man prays to the Lord for the work to be done by the government.

If the will (inborn memory-Sitham) is completely filled with faith, there will be very little room for desires.

Desires do not go away cleanly. Therefore, pure renunciation is not possible, it is materialistic.

A car that came fast near... distracted the thought.

I was walking fast in the shadow of the roadside.

For money transactions and choice of goods, knowledge first seeks the perceived knowledge (inborn memory). Due to their ignorance of the price, the pictures and images imprinted on their memory are the first tools for them to buy the goods.

This is the first reason for poor and rich appearances. Asking to buy a product worth a thousand even if it costs ten thousand!

He who loses money becomes poor.

Needs are determined by the will enriched by desires, inborn out of previous birth cause and effect resultant.

The price of a product without any kind of prior experience is an empty image at will. Immediately one of the seeds of desire sprouts and tells the knowledge of the unnecessary nature of its needs.

In the shadow of the night, the cold was pleasant.

The silence was resounding.

I entered the house again.

I folded the meditation seat and drank some hot water.

The body heat was eating away the cold outside little by little.

30 years of dieting, starting work with coffee in the morning.

A very small amount of vegetable rice in the afternoon.

With any fruits at night, my diet completely affected my alimentary tract affected by Corona. Then the American banana tree burned in December and then sprouted in March and changed my alimentary tract.

And travel makes the body crave to taste new food. The diet has changed in the last six months.

There is no doubt that food is the first step to spirituality.

Right food always carries balanced air in the body and meditation. Meditation is always flowing in the body. It is only noticed when we sit as if we are meditating! Like looking at the stars...

All beings have knowledge. That knowledge controls the decision-making, intellect mind like a rope holding the will at one end and the ego at the other.

All these are powered by a battery that is concentrated by the cosmic force of life. Although life is not as transcendental as cosmic energy, it has the semblance of cosmic energy because it comes through the universe.

But life itself cannot know the ability to choose, learn or know, anything.

In life, we always need a teacher to learn. And that teacher is always the cosmic power—God.

Cosmic power acts with life as unified oneness (in Tamil Ondrai). Feel the sensations through the senses.

Life also needs a "light for the eyes to see" any object. It is the characteristic of differential or supporter (in Tamil Vaerai).

God lives as a companion of life. That is, even if life does any action due to its own desire, the Lord, the universal power is needed to consume that action(in Tamil Udanaai).

So, in the nature of life, together as COMPANION.

Others as a TEACHER or SUPPORTER.

With you as a CONSUMER or LIFELINE.

The Lord, the universal force of existence is always present in all living beings.

Where are places of worship?

As the symbolic representative of God pervades all the life-sensing tools.

For all beings, knowledge manifests the power in the direction of desire.

Inborn knowledge sends the impulse in the same direction as the gun of the ego stands!

That's why most of the decisions vary from person to person and a number of products are manufactured. The product varies because the decisions are different!

Prices are set in a place of "ignorance" when a lot of goods are in short supply.

One starts believing what the seller says about the product.

For example, if one wants to buy turmeric or turmeric powder, he buys it even if it costs a hundred times more when it is not freely available.

Such is one's impression of the will—inborn knowledge about the need for turmeric.

Decision-making is defined, on the one hand as a decision from a collection of knowledge and on the other, from a collection of experiences.

In the collection of experiences, the experiences of worshiping desire, the general characteristic of life, are recorded.

When there is no desire, the movement of life ceases.

The elimination of desire and the reduction of desire can happen with the help of knowledge. But that too is done by the inborn imprints of desire way.

Controlling desire means keeping the body, mind, and intellect healthy.

It can happen by considering the condition.

Uncontrollable desire surpasses virtue, morality, and dharma, even if there are records in the will of that person, throwing everything away, life runs towards desire!

That is, the ego is energized by the inborn desire imprints to experience the cause and effect of deeds already done, and just God sees that the resultant experience is going through by the present life as per its deeds.

God runs like a man with a calf to enjoy that desire!

God's power works intending to somehow enjoy that desire in this life and leave it empty, resting, and returning to a state of peace.

Since knowledge has the nature of decision-making, it decides the direction of inborn desire and can experience the pre-born cause, effect, and fruition.

Even life without any record of inborn desire imprints determines their need for food.

Not all living things eat the same food.

Not all birds eat the same type of fruit.

Not all livestock eat only vegetative foods.

This nature of birth also proves that economic inequalities are normal in society.

Such economic disparities lead to poverty and disease, hindering a society from moving towards a higher civilization.

It is only because of the control of this society and the government that the man who is driven by that desire can succeed and lead a better life.

Even when all the information is published and there is no "ignorance", in democracy, he votes for the one who will help him and fulfill his "desires" despite virtue, dharma, and morality.

Knowledge chooses him, even if he is an unethical man whom he knows, who can help him, then a man who leads a virtuous life with whom he is not acquainted.

It is because of the innate desire derived from inborn desire imprints.

Boring today… Different kinds of thoughts are distracting me.…

Where did you go?

It seems to be walking away as always.

Well…well…off the busy road and into the interior.

I started walking on the cement pavement near the ground on a quiet road.

The great power of this world is working as knowledge; all the scholars have told this fact!

What seems to me to be true is that knowledge gained through experience is the best knowledge.

Logical knowledge gained through information seems to fit cause-and-effect results and causes a lot of ignorance.

Because acquiring such knowledge requires financial implications.

Adversely this economic scarcity increases the intensity of desire.

How to use any app and what information can be obtained is knowledge. It removes part of ignorance (all share market frauds).

Even if the ignorance is removed…

Ignorance prevails over the one who does not have the necessary material.

Poverty comes to him because he cannot overcome his ignorance of the original "price"—so

scarcity is coming.

Whenever scarcity prevails unless virtue, morality and dharma are not legally imposed on him to make up for whatever lack there is, the speed of the egoic impulse of desire makes him overstep everything and thus an individual terrorist is created.

Such a radical man becomes the enemy of the living beings who are moving towards the goal of higher civilization for the group he lives in and the groups he belongs to.

Knowledge of the Supreme Universal Power is necessary for every living being.

Knowledge constructed from information is distinctly different quality from perception.

The divine universal power has unique eight qualities that I have studied. And in my experience, I feel that is true!

Universal energy is not created by man. Universal energy knows the information of what and where and how any actions of this world are happening in all areas.

(Man seeks, probes and knows information only with others' help).

Cosmic power has a great level of knowledge!

An organism's stomach knows how much acid it should secrete to digest any food. Is it not an act of God?

The moment any creature dies, the biodegrading organisms come out from the dormant state that it has been living in that same creature. How miraculous?

God has created power.

What an amazing thing!

Universal power is the great benevolent power.

It has given all the climatic conditions necessary for life to live happily. It has given food, oxygen and other life-supporting gases which support its life force.

Universal power does not have any obstacles like desire, arrogance, etc. to attain divine status.

There is no place without cosmic energy. Because where there is life, cosmic energy must come from there.

Universal power is a great power because the entire weight of this world is floating in this universe. So, he is the one who supports this world.

Universal power is the reason everyone wants that great peaceful, blissful state that living beings can experience. Cosmic energy has no form; it is absolute power.

It is the desire to always enjoy that peace and blissful state that made people create different types of religious worship.

A disciplined state of life and unchanging remembrance of the universe can attain a state of unbroken connection with cosmic power while living.

In other words, it may be compared with the inbuilt battery in the cell phone; just like the external battery is charged externally, all living beings have a divine state as an inbuilt battery, but when they are connected with cosmic power through body, mind, ego, intellect, and memory are all harmoniously, silently without any seeking and just aware of the existence in cosmic power get to know the existence of the God as energy.

There are also different types of enrichment.

Today my mind is light. It is pleasant. What is the reason?

I don't know. Leave the man!

The knowledge and thought processes are basically run as per the direction of inborn desires imprinted in our brains.

Our brain can shun a thought when erupts. But most of the time our lack of awareness causes us to run behind our thought.

But most of the time we are always running in the flow of thought born out of a lack of awareness about ourselves.

Anxieties, desires, hatred, love, affection and gratitude are all dependent on this type.

When we push aside unnecessary thoughts, we are left with only emptiness. Spirituality or lust immediately takes over that place.

Our ancestors, therefore, say - in a different way - that mantra chanting helps to control the movement of thought!

Even after my religious initiation, I could not be completely residing in Shiva's thoughts. Shivogam!

But I am always thinking of Shiva and chanting his name.

But the "Wholeness" is the problem. I doubt how my " life energy " and " cosmic power" blending is not fully happening all time.

When there is no wholeness there is void space prevailing.

TV channels, multi-media and all other entertainment are filling the void very cleverly.

It is the movements of desires that drive us to the Tamasa Guna, Rajho Guna, and Sattva Guna (laziness, highly motivated and a perfect state of peace).

Desire drives the mind as a vehicle and knowledge as energy.

The only thing that bothers me the most is,

Spiritual practice alone is not enough for this world.

A person undergoing this spiritual training can be a fully active spiritualist only if he has financial independence and complacency.

When it comes to economic comfort, it is related to inborn desires.

When spirituality is different and worldly life is different, we have to be false to both.

Knowledge is the only weapon we have.

It is from this arsenal of knowledge that we can carve out our lives. I don't know if that knowledge has freedom. Because if knowledge is empirical knowledge, it is bound to the cause and effect of previous actions (whether in previous birth or recent past) from the cosmic power. It is controlled only by cosmic power.

So, knowledge is a slave to cosmic power.

When this understanding comes, the ego is somewhat understood, and we can take control of it.

The ego does not go away. One can reduce the intensity of ego, through true devotion to God and voracious seeking to remove the inborn desire imprints.

The knowledge created based on the information is only used to inflate the ego.

It is used to increase desire and promote hatred, love, and affection.

Only when the age-old imprints of lust are regulated by morality, there can be a start toward higher social civilization.

It seems to me that if a man loves a woman all the time, he is lying.

At one time, when the lustful mind comes across the image of another woman, it secretly falls in love with her too.

Here morality, ethics, dharma, and restrictions are to be imposed by the government to prevent any lustful action is taking place .

Otherwise, the seed of desire and lustful power start to act in violation of knowledge.

A united family system and a stamp of status for the family is a fence to his knowledge. No crime is committed willingly. The reason is the seeds of desire embedded in knowledge. Virtue, morals, and dharma are required to prevent it from sprouting.

Today, I came from Jacksonville to Atlanta County via Georgia. It was very cold. We stayed at a hotel with our daughter, son-in-law, and grandchildren. As always, I meditated since dawn.

The prominent assignment of knowledge is to protect one's ego.

The ego seems to have one type of love for those around it and another type of love for others.

So is hatred.

Money is the main tool to express love. Since knowledge works on the one hand touching the memory and on the other side ego, the ego forces the knowledge to fulfill the desires recorded in the will through pre-birth. This is why love is expressed in a biased, one-sided, and spreads discrimination.

The true state of love transcends knowledge.

It is beyond one's inborn memory. It embraces cosmic unbiased love, full of forgiveness, full of discrimination. There is no space for information-based knowledge and or inborn memory-based knowledge.

Impeccable true love of God is expressed by imposing self-punishment by most people.

But any being in the state of unequivocal true love never discriminates. The love defined for man is the love within the boundaries of protecting his social group, community, and country.

True love, never see partiality.

Management cannot function without diversity.

A society cannot be guided by exoneration and impunity.

Virtue, morality, and dharma can be upheld in a society where criminals are punished.

So, the level of understanding of individual human love and the level of understanding of community love should be different.

So, this universe made of love is God.

Only a person who realizes himself as a unique person can go along with his goal and succeed.

Thus, being pleasant, comforting, loving, loyal, and spreading gratitude are states of mind differentiated into the self-personality state of egoism.

Therefore, love, compassion, gratitude, and love mixed with respect is called Bhakti.

The Lord gives mercy to the killer and forgives those with deadly arrogance. Some of those arrogant people are forgiven if their previous birth, cause, and effect results are good to those people who lead comfortable lives now.

God's power never discriminates to provide rain, food, or shelter to a murderer or a person with good deeds. It continues its course in the state of impartial, unbiased supreme love. Everyone gets sunlight and fresh air.

I need some clarification…

Understood… Understood…

The mercy and love of nature and the universe cannot be fully expressed by human beings in a managerial point of position.

That is why religions and creeds are isolated. True divine individuality is distorted by the individual human personality and egos. And materiality takes its place as a commodity for love and mercy.

Hmmm…I don't understand a bit… Okay!

Be that as it may, I will say what I say. What?

Man has created the structure of social groups that cannot realize divine status without economic support.

Accordingly, the eight qualities of God, are inscribed in the will of human beings, i.e., living beings as per their effective capacity. God never assigns all of his eight qualities. He deserves few for his own.

Active knowledge and ego can only depend on material wealth.

So…

Can't a loving, kind, human live peacefully?

Who will feed a man who does not work, earn money, or have property?

Who will be comforted? Those who flatter them and comfort them do not do so in the absence of expectations.

At least they are doing it with the expectation of some kind of stance that their sins will be removed, merit will accrue, atonement, etc.

The government should protect people who are suffering from these old, sick, bad habit-prone persons, but those government employees allotted the job are not doing it in true love. They do it as boring work.

That's right...

Although the sun came down well, the cold was intense. We sat in an empty building next to our door...

How are you?

He laughed lightly. Sun, cold, wind, darkness, light, all these things change the actions of living beings.

Yes, yes...

I want to know something!

What?

Is knowledge true?

No. When knowledge comes as information, images are imprinted as images according to one's desire.

This is the weapon of politicians in a democracy. A misrepresentation by someone about someone or an event.

Even ten percent of people who browse through information will not check its veracity. They keep saying that the information is true, that they have heard it, that they know it, or something like that.

Experiential or innate knowledge, i.e., inborn knowledge, is true. All other knowledge derived from logic is false, unexamined and untested rather than false.

I've often thought that even in the process of copulation, it is often a fantasy or wishful thinking phenomenon.

That's why Vedanta tells us to discard everything saying, "This is unnecessary for me." Such assigned innate qualities of desire are very helpful to a journey towards a certain goal.

For example, if a student who sits down to prepare for an exam today has thoughts of lust or addiction, if he learns to set aside that I don't need it now, he can focus on studying and do it completely and carefully.

But the sufferer, pulled by thoughts, puts down the book and runs after the distracting thoughts. Losing!

Does one need it or not? The man has to do the security check.

The oath of segregating the good for self-development helps to progress spiritually—makes the vehicle for achieving the goal of zeal run smoothly.

A security check of the knowledge runs in line with desire. A student's desire to go to a job makes him study well.

He studies without distraction.

The zeal of a person who wants to be a political leader makes him pretend to be a caregiver and he willingly does it. He does not give up on this goal (agenda) no matter how big his work is. He solemnly affirms to attend all of his loyalists' functions and ceremonies.

What you came to say is very simple! Knowledge is false! It is also created through desire.

It is evening time. The yellow was tinged with red. Birds were flying in the sky.

Even though there was less traffic, I could not hear the sound of vehicles, but many trucks and cars were driving in the distance.

I believe that the natural qualities of life like knowledge, desire, and action can be controlled through training the life force through pranayamam (breathing exercises) that I have been dwelling on.

Even though we have brought desires through the will of birth, we can cut off unwanted thoughts in a moment, even if we continuously implement these desires through knowledge, ego, and mind.

But most of the time we have thoughts, we are unconsciously running behind them...

When the remembrance of the past is crossing me, usually it is painful and I am used to cutting off the thoughts that bother me as soon as I don't want them.

Instead, immediately chanting the name of the Lord makes me visualize the images of the Lord.

I choose the image of God according to my mood.

The tank of willed memory transmits from one place—what the world says about good or bad.

That is, it is not a bee that only eats honey, it is like a fly that also sits on dung and honey.

For this, they must learn to sit only on honey and strengthen themselves for themselves, without any concern for the world.

So, what you are saying is that knowledge binds us.

Yes, knowledge is the ego identifying me, which has the resemblances of the God of cosmic power that energized my life to experience the cause-and-effect resultants.

Life is like God who has no origin and end.

A substance without birth and death like the Lord that pervades everything!

Its quality is knowledge, desire, and action, and this is together known as life.

It is the rays of thought that emancipate from inborn desire-driven knowledge, and action that manifest one's character.

Of the two tools it touches, the will (Sitham) and the ego (Agangaram), the ego is the self-consciousness that when trained can stop the signals of any thought.

For example, a crying baby could be diverted to be calm by showing something. Similarly, adults can also stop or stimulate both painful and pleasurable thinking.

It has started getting dark.

I got up and started walking…

I wake up at 3 am.

I meditated for a while. My mind was clear.

Although we understand that the innate sense of knowledge which is the foundation of knowledge, Information knowledge emerges in line with Inborn knowledge.

Both knowledges are designed by God to experience the pain and pleasure it is bound to experience due to previous birth cause and effect resultant.

The inborn knowledge based on desires gets its experience by utilizing the information-based knowledge built in due course very strategically.

When this powerful inborn desire should not harm other beings, it must be controlled by ethics, discipline, and Dharma through stringent laws and punishment.

Ego with training has the power to control knowledge by enriching it or deactivating the velocity.

Correcting knowledge as controlling its movement, can be done through ego, knowledge can operate with intensity to emancipate to higher itself, but everything is done through innate experience, cause and effect, and resultant record.

Therefore, the legal systems of a society should be designed to protect the freedom of the individual (ego)human life.

At the same time, virtue, dharma, and non-harmful conditions for other living beings should be built through government laws.

Why do you care?

Yes…

Why do I care?

Religions and the cult of groups have to become institutions. And as long as they are institutions, there must be a business in them.

Because economic freedom is what it takes.

But such religions and religious institutions should not leave the pursuit of wealth construction as the path of economic development.

Secondly, man has the maturity to automatically eliminate the experience of what he perceives as obstacles to the realization of divinity.

Desire is the second quality of life. The desire for food, sexual intercourse, sleep, and to take political leadership personality. The inborn desire is a vital part to experience the cause and effect of previous life's resultants.

For all the actions of man, knowledge, will, and ego are operating by receiving the signals from the record of this inborn desire imprints.

Information-based knowledge includes the fields of language, science, self-awareness, religion, morality, and society in education. The origin and development of each must depend on these and it should be taught.

The development of knowledge depends on the strength of the natural birth impressions. Entire life experiences are based on the inborn desire impression.

Therefore, social laws and order systems give man freedom of life, freedom of knowledge, freedom of desire, and freedom of action, and make him the superior and economically wealthy and self-respecting society with freedom of a well-built ego.

The inborn urge of desire for sexual intercourse while moving towards a higher quality of civilization ethics, discipline, and dharma are to be adopted and taught. The resultant form is the "family system" concocted by our ancestors. I believe of the entire living things kingdom humans are adopting this system as an emancipation of higher civilization where trust between the couples is emphasized and they behave with others as brothers and sisters.

It is now being shattered by the porno makers and people with little knowledge about ethics, and discipline is grossly violated as there is little control by law.

The biggest businesses in the world are centered around inducing such innate desires.

One cannot attain God if one has lustful thoughts.

There are spiritual thoughts about God that love is the center of family life.

Morality, morals, dharma, etc., are the rules to bring this inborn lust within a definition.

They are brought into society and those who violate it are punished through laws. Murders relating to lust are going on all the time.

Now, this inborn desire can be regulated by society only through moral education. Crimes can be deterred only by severely punishing the violators.

If a higher standard of society has to be created in civilization, economy and spirituality, the understanding of the nature of life must be given to man through experience.

Fasting methods can also preserve and sustain this healthy body through discipline. Man should realize that.

Ignorance is the lifeblood of desires. Be it food preferences, or a desire for sensual pleasure,

The experience gained when the optimization of energy of the body is disturbed and the body is harmed by disease, reduces the level of these desires.

But since these preferences are birth records, they start sprouting again.

A restrictive family environment can be the only solution to reduce these preferences in society.

Imprints of learned desires often go along with his innate desires.

Man does not like to experience something he does not like. When he thinks that the pleasure derived from such desire is not painful to him, he develops those desires more and more.

In it, education is the desire for information, physical labor is the desire to materialize the talent, or the desire to express oneself as a talented person through work, and the desire to sleep in hallucination facing the moments that occur through drugs.

I wake up at midnight. I slowly came and sat in the hall.

Is birth good? Is it bad? Why did our ancestors say no to human birth?

They said that to be born as a human requires great penance!

At the same time, they also said that there should be a great life without birth.

Both sound right to me!

But life is contradicted by economic well-being and healthy relationship. Both are existing as desire stands underneath. Desire to live out of diseases. Attitudes that cannot accept old age have started crying to the Lord, the universal power, saying that there should not be birth again.

But wealth creation even though falls under the cycle of "raise" "stands" and "perish" is an indispensable bridge to connect wealth creation activities and human-related activities. So, everyone prays and seeks God to provide wealth. Ultimately, we believe that abundant wealth will solve most of our problems.

If we have sufficient material, we can dissolve all the dangers of life.

We have the belief that those who have experienced it say that the Lord, the cosmic power, is conglomerate at the living beings so that they can stand together with the cosmic power and enjoy the pleasure while forgetting themselves and their feelings.

Such divinity does not give pleasure only at the level of individual consciousness and it cannot be the path to the highest level of human civilization, because only those who deny matter and consider human energy as a mere instrument can have the connection of divinity.

If a man cries to God that he wants a blissful life without birth, God does not allow us to be born in a social environment beyond our control.

My thinking is that if one accepts birth willingly and lives in a prosperous society and can be born again and again and experience pleasures and pains, then the state of suffering is…

…dependent on funding. It is believed that one who is in a prosperous economic position can simultaneously achieve godliness and a high level of social civilization.

But human inborn birth desires, ego, and self-consciousness always create differences and imbalances among human beings. The self-consciousness of ego never makes a person equal. If this is done equally, man's ability to work and get a job will disappear and all living beings will be in other states of lust and drug addiction.

For a noble, uncivilized society, God's mercy, forgiving nature, the nature of doing the work with dedication as the will of God, a rich economy, legal programs that control and regulate desires, and the environment for egoism and freedom of experience should be considered as the highest level of civilization.

If it is possible, the answer is yes and no.

Because wherever there are potential elements to bring the states of life like knowledge, desire, actions, will, intellect, ego, and mind under a control, only there lies the key to superior civilization.

I woke up as usual at 3 am. After meditating, I looked through the porthole window towards the highway. Freight trains were plying and the vehicular traffic was light.

Imagination is the images experienced in the will that are expanded into a different model, real (original) for a different scene.

The seed of imagination is in the will.

The seed of desire is recorded in inborn birth memory and a record of information-based knowledge experience.

An ant can be imagined as a huge elephant.

But man cannot imagine anything without any experience.

All imagination requires experience.

Sometimes when you imagine without experience, it is likely to be pre-birth impressions. Imaginations are often lustful and images and words that have given us painful experiences often come to the fore...

When these impressions come out in the body, all the chemicals that are secreted in the body when those impressions, images, and real experiences come, are re-secreted.

We consider them to be concerned with painful experiences.

Innate erotic impressions and experiential erotic impressions are responsible for erotic upheaval. Commercials without women and other TV programs and entertainment features are designed to relieve people from anxiety and make them not think in a different way or for personal growth leading to a higher standard of living.

Egoism is understood in various forms. The first manifestation of ego is the cry after the birth of a baby. The purpose of the ego is to make others aware of the state of existence.

This is denied in theology. Existence is the only substance, Vyapakam(omnipresent), Brahmam, or Shiva.

When that is the case, the condition of living beings is also within this Vyapakam(wholeness).

When it is like that, the condition of living beings is also in this Vyapakam. When it is like that, some people think that one can realize the state of God without ego.

But the state of Brahmam is identified by the ego itself, and through knowledge it conveys to life.

No two babies are born at the same time, the same microsecond in a hospital without a change of geographical place, their…

Horoscopes would certainly be identical, but in reality, no two children are alike. Their education, position, happiness, and suffering are necessarily different.

What we know from this is that the cause of birth, cause-effect benefit, and cause for a new life is imparted to the respective lives through knowledge, and its life is determined from the decisions taken by the respective lives.

I don't know if existentialism noticed this. But the sense of existence itself is identified by knowledge and in turn conveyed to the consciousness of life.

The nature of the ego is always biased. It pompously adds value to one's life and makes itself known to others that they are big. The ego never underestimates it.

The root cause of likes and dislikes is the ego's inherent discriminating nature.

God is without a beginning and end, life too has no beginning and end.

It is God's grace to grant the body life according to its cause-and-effect resultants.

.No one can eradicate ego. As long as there is God, there will be life.

As long as there is life, there will be ego.

Everyone sees the ego as an evil thing.

We aim to bring about a higher human civilization by uniting the powerful ego with divine power.

The highest social civilization in which man completely understands that any act on this earth is done by God is the highest civilization in the world. In India, most of the ancient temples with intrinsic workmanship do not have an identity of the maker.

The identity of a human doer is not visible to anyone. But respecting the ego of the individual is a need of this hour to build a higher civilization.

The ego is the identity of human life, which is the manifestation of the giving body, the sensory organs as tools, and the geographical area and experience in which that life has to undergo based on the cause and effect of previous birth results.

Even though there are so many pieces of literature, scriptures, and teachers to propagate ethics, discipline, and dharma to the people.

Desires are what drive the ego. It is egoism that disturbs sleep.

Making and using commodities is egoism.

The ego is a very short-spaced stage, a stage before the divine stage.

The wonder is that ego is helping us to unite with God!

The state without ego is the state of death. If a creation is to be created to leave a trace of its existence in this world, the reason is man's greed acting through ego.

But if the creation exists without making known the name of the creator, then it becomes the creation of God.

But all creation takes place within God's pervasiveness (Vyabagam).

Cosmic power is the root cause of these creations.

The superior society of civilization divinely regulates this egoism, makes identities disappear, and such groups and institutions disappear very soon because any creation is distinguished by the work of the group's ego, the work of the institution, I believe, has to flag the promoter and vital person. His ego then serves as the synergy of God and humans' joint work.

Knowledge, desire, and action are the nature of life and to manifest these as action, the small cosmic power called ego (Agangaram) binds itself to its will (Sitham), and knowledge. It ends up in the invisible medium/tool called the mind which is made up of chemical compounds emitting powerful electromagnetic signals at the speed of microlight.

The ego is the cause of economic production and the development of spirituality on the other hand.

While one is running, the other needs to be hidden. As the central point for both levels, moral, ethical, and strict laws are the answer to this.

Even if you do that, egoism belongs to God because it is a property of life.

God does not harm living beings as He is bound by the eight qualities enriched with mercy and love.

One's suffering is caused by the cause and effect of action-results of life.

Just as the chemical processes occur in the body precisely, God directs the universe into the intellect, designing the cause and effect of resultant benefits appropriate to the activities of the living beings to be enjoyed by the respective living beings engraved in the Karana and Sariram—cause for the need of a body to the "life."

It is beyond the power of human understanding.

Therefore, worshiping the Lord is manifested as a prayer, compliments, complaints, and tremours born out of pure love to help lives to experience these pleasures and pains without difficulty and have evolved into devotional literature.

A story will be told to explain this. In a town, a person was giving food to the poor. One day, when he was bringing the food, an eagle carried a poisonous snake in the sky, and the venom of the snake got into the food and many people who ate the food died.

Another day, some people inquired about where the almsgiving was taking place in that town. When they asked an old woman who kept a shop on that street corner, she identified the house and mentioned the recent incident and said that there is a house of a person who gives food with poison. Those who came for alms left the place without taking food.

Now, the question arises who will bear the sin? Is it the person who has given alms, the poisonous snake, or the eagle that carried it?

The story ends as the Lord said, "The old woman who spread rumors about this sinful incident has to bear the fruit of her sinful action."

The subtle cause and effect are the result whether good or bad deeds are compressed into the Karana Sariram (cause for taking the body) by God.

It is the primary grace of God to show inactivated life in a dormant state to whom this reason for taking birth is declared, to experience, and enjoy life and reach the godly state.

The sky was clear and the sound of the night was mixed with the light of the moon.

What do you mean?

For me, egoism becomes the reality of worldly life.

Man needs full knowledge of the divine state and full knowledge of the ego to realize the divine state of this ego which is a hindrance to the realization of the divine state.

The ego always pretends that it does not exist. Be proactive and try to push yourself forward.

To differentiate oneself from others, the first step is to level up others who see other people's faults and make stealthy efforts to rise above!

The ego tries to sow division everywhere because of its natural character!

Egoism perpetuates fake love!

Cheating, deceiving, dishonesty, disloyalty, setting up a group against the enemy as a friend's group, etc. will continue to do all efforts without stopping!

The ego always requires compliments!

But none of these are among the eight attributes of God.

On the contrary, compassion and forgiveness are qualities that help a person reduce the intensity of ego.

How can a society run peacefully if it condones the thief and those who commit the most brutal acts?

So, in this place morals and worldly life separate.

God never punishes any living being, but only its cause-and-effect resultants punish the doer now or then.

The Lord is providing an undiminished flood of happiness to living beings.

But egoism is a hindrance to enjoying it!

Depression is a disability of the ego!

Ignorance is the state of not properly understanding the living and pushing it to the state of depression!

People with such depression can improve themselves.

But as they are craving pleasure, they do things for preparing themselves to come from depression.

Ego strives to express itself!

It wants to express itself in some way like its name, image, style, and family. So, gifting a shawl, saluting, smiling, clapping, etc. are kept as rituals to satisfy it.

Driven by desire, egoism has acquired the ability to mix readily with all living beings!

But as soon as it is mixed, it observes the actions of others!

It starts to look out for others' fallacies. It assigns great care to find the faults of others, which ultimately builds strength to ego and thereby identifies their weaknesses, and makes sure of the differences!

The ego is helpful to shape and manage work, so it is the root cause of economic development. Because of ego, man is unable to achieve the state of love and mercy, so only if the state of godliness and economic sentiment is balanced, a superior civilization can be developed.

A model that can satisfy the personal growth of man and also satisfy the pride of social groups.

In today's society, it is imperative that the personal adornment of the ego is freedom. Social egoism too is to enjoy freedom, which is true freedom, but there should not be any violation of morals, violation of virtue, or corruption of dharma.

I came out of meditation wherein moderate lighting is pervading.

Ignorance, what is the purpose of God giving a body to the living beings lying in the darkness?

Love, love, love.

Mercy! Mercy! Mercy!

It is in this power that the Lord appears. Just like the mushroom seeds that were condensing in the bark of the tree emerging with the rain, living beings also take the body when the right moment comes.

A sense of transcendence and the understanding that God is our guide and that each of our energies is different but that is the bridge to connect us must develop.

Those who seek to realize and experience Godliness forever are unable to fully engage to produce material production, economic development, and economic security.

Therefore, asceticism is a state of renunciation of desire. One who renounces a loved one is ascetic, which is a powerful weapon to enrich knowledge to realize God. This ultimately strengthens one to segregate himself from the group.

But if this process is taken up by the group to balance seeking godliness along with material wealth creation it will pave way for a higher standard of civilization.

It is a weapon to strengthen the knowledge of God through knowledge. This was revealed to the world by Mahatma Gandhi and Nelson Mandela.

God-conscious people are forgiving and merciful at all costs, but they are used for business purposes from an economic point of view.

Two different and conflicting states of the orderly state of God consciousness can be brought together to create a superior civilized society.

In the evening sun, the sky was slowly swallowing the sun with red petals.

The golden blue sky was slowly swaying. A sparrow on the tip of a branch flew towards the next tree.

Inborn desire imprints in the memory tank cause a chemical change in the body, which triggers electronic signals and expands into the mind.

Mind is an instrument under our control through Sitham (inborn memory tank of the being), on one end Agangaram (ego), and knowledge in the next immediate level.

But the operating instructions are not under our control.

God's action does not destroy these registers.

We are just an instrument.

The awareness that the universe is doing something through us will help us to slow down the reaction.

Information collected by sensory organs is passed on to inborn knowledge desires and information knowledge desires which process those inputs and the resultants are normally based on inborn recorded desires.

Otherwise, the sensory organ signals are kept safely as pictures in the inborn memory tank.

For example, if there is candy on the table when you wake up in the morning, the passer-by can take it and secure it somewhere or leave it there.

After two days, when a child comes home, he remembers the candy and takes it for himself because he took it when he was alone. If not, he asks where it was on the table and takes it.

When the signals from knowledge come from an amputee patient, although there is a chemical change there, the mind is unable to do anything because the limbs are not understood.

But when there is the same chemical production due to the intensity of the desire, the patient himself tries to complete it with the help of some other person.

The shape of the mind is the shape of desires! The speed of the mind is the speed of desires!

The nature of life, knowledge, and desires do not function without life. They are non-living material things. Similarly, when knowledge and desires do not work, the ego does not work.

So, the mind ceases to exist.

If the mind is in a superior state, then the knowledge is in the cosmic power of God.

It drives the impulses and desires, and those impulses drive the ego, and it becomes the mind—not constantly, but only at those moments.

If all the senses are screened, then knowledge, desire, and ego will be suppressed only if the mind, life's knowledge, desire, and will, which are related to the ego, are stopped. The mind will also be depressed.

Therefore, the universal power of God is imprinted repeatedly in the mind, and they are embedded as experiences and are a rich storehouse of divine qualities.

But when the inborn Godly impressions are low against the predatory power in the same mind, in whatever divine environment those people are, their knowledge and desires, their ego and desires fly away as money-seeking evil.

Worships, rituals and societies have been established over time as ways to forcefully impose this divine power of God as life's Inbuilt battery

Slowly, I came out of meditation.

I was not able to meditate fully as before because the idea of writing a book is coming together from time to time in my brain.

As always, the light of the night was surrounded by a flow of thoughts.

I did not feel that there is a good mind and a bad mind. The mind acts accordingly. The information through the experience is different and the information from birth is different. When vigor is subtracted from whatever is heavier, the intensity of the sign is definitely reduced. That end result can be obtained differently.

I am least bothered about literature comforting entertainment. All media and most prints are doing this only.

Nowadays, I am less concerned about my body. When I was very concerned about my body, the cosmic energy was very concerned about me. We were together. When I am traveling towards economic development, the cosmic energy understanding the body's electrovalence left me uninterrupted and looking at us, to leave us, independently to experience the birth way pain or pleasure during the venture.

During this time, our cosmic power regrets our selection of running behind money orientation.

Knowledge and energy are debated. Cosmic energy does not like debate at all.

It is the cosmic force in the form of great mercy that says, "Let me be the loser. You be the winner and leave me in the noise of the market that I can't fully know the bliss of peace."

In me, the universal divine power is fully diffused only when it is the subtle impotence of Agangaram. This is what we call "surrender." In the journey to socio-economic prosperity, this surrender is obedience imposed on the laborers at the place of employment.

I had a wonderful meditation today. The body is very light. There is a soft tingling sensation on the scalp. As always! The smell of late night…There is a weed….

The cause of poverty is ignorance and ignorance of management. Human power is the most beautiful creation of the universe. All human records are records of loving, compassionate, concentrated energy.

All the countries of the world should come under one administration. To realize the eternal cosmic power of God requires the proper training methods to experience. Whatever the qualities of the man are, the methods of training should be set up according to him. That is the best human civilization. Virtue, morals, Dharma and ethics in human life should be taught and disciplined through punishments.

All laws require that the fine and penalty be revised every five years, according to inflation and corporal punishment.

The fact that poverty has not been eradicated for so long as human civilization has developed is a sign of the selfish arrogance of governments.

And a group's egos are not recognized by other groups. Punishment should be given within three days, whatever the offences are.

All men are willing to work. There should be a unification of individual ego and communal ego. He should be given a task that is towards achieving a single goal.

An individual human ego with a wrong goal is invalid. In that deviation, laziness and lustful impressions in the inborn desire gain momentum.

Artificial intelligence (AI) is a manifestation of the social ego, a set of human egos.

This artificial intelligence will definitely help in the governance of the entire human race.

God has not created anything on this earth that is not needed by mankind. All living and non-living things are created to enable the experience of their cause-and-effect results.

To experience the states of happiness and suffering they are created.

By virtues, morals, dharma and uniform ego by which the world seeks material gain by maintaining ignorance.

Because only materials can fulfill the inborn desires of a man very elegantly. False information to spread ignorance is spread in the name of freedom of expression. Family and public information should be limited to certain or proven facts or conjecture (logical).

Egoism, unpolished by virtue, creates divisions everywhere.

The egos of groups must be recognized.

But the law and its dharma must be common.

The gross production output is the group's ego output which is to be divided by the group's constituent numbers. The price of the output is to be fixed based on the result.

There is no such thing as waste products, that do not have any demand. If someone says that the product has no value it is ignorance, some have a demand for the product.

Man does not produce anything unnecessarily. When all goods and services are available to everyone, there will be no such thing as a fake market.

World narcotic drug production divided by world population is very small. It is the individual ego that is running the violent black-market work that is carried on the backs of the people to eke out their livelihood and food to eat every day.

When it becomes the ego of the group, the government, the light will come into that dark market. People will get food and medicine.

When we share comprehensive information technology with all the people of the world, we can eliminate "ignorance" to some extent. Chat GPT powered by Artificial Intelligence (AI) and LaMDA Dale should not be anti-theocratic.

It should also be considered a part of the development of modern civilization.

Science cannot grow without spirituality and both should never conflict.

The Lord who resides in living beings is of holy nature of the Universal Lord.

Identify the objects with the help of universal power different from living things and help living things to gain knowledge, hence God is residing as differently.

And God lives within us as action through the body all along.

By these means, human beings are of the same holiness as God. Real truth is what every human ego realizes.

If the excellence of human civilization is to be understood as divine grace, non-attachment of desires, and a power of great bliss, it must apply to the whole of human society.

The human ego has group-to-group boundaries as every house has boundaries.

Total expenditure on defense is antithetical to high civilization.

Savage human egoism seems to be the same as the use of a weapon investment—the use of a country.

Because all the weapons for the security of the countries of the world are used only for the protection of human morality, discipline, and dharma, a regulated human ego is possible.

The development of science should be such that the ego of man is similar to the ego of the group, the ego of the group is compatible with the ego of other groups and generally accepts God.

While comparing domestic violence, gang violence, and national violence, it all boils down to "ignorance."

Every human being is a form of divine, dynamic, sacred power, but because his ego is not known to him, his power turns to ignorance, violence, and anti-egoism of socially undesirable groups in response to receiving love.

The real high civilization is to enrich what is inherent in man, to transform it into an ego that is useful and suitable for society. The falsehood of isolation that God is holy must be overcome. Those are his limited powers.

The atom can be fissioned into an infinite form of energy like ego too, that when synergically conglomerate can enrich society.

Considering "ignorance" as a demand, the government should stop the companies that produce goods and services towards this demand.

For this, there should be a single global authority and its distribution of power to nations and groups.

Individual egoism and group egoism differ in one place and that is "forgiveness." It should be punished by understanding the truth of cause-and-effect action and consequence.

There is nothing without a cause. So, things in this world are happening because of some reason. We need to get the information and knowledge to accept it.

The mind was blank... It was three at night.

I was the only one in the room.

He asked me gently.

That's right. Why did the sages and ancestors hate this human birth and say they don't want another birth?

He spoke.

I tilted my head a bit. Some sages want it and some sages don't.

The Lord bestows this human birth on the measure of the cause-and-effect resultants. No life will escape from the results of their actions either in this current life span or in their past life. It is the ultimate Grace of God. He never fails to leave a life without results. So, human life is highest in the form and subtle energy it is granted to those who deserve it to experience good and bad and surrender to God as he is the creator, maintainer and destroyer (absorber).

In this birth, sages who find that they are given the best opportunity to grasp Him after suffering innumerable pain to shun their sensory pleasure to find peace in God, find that this life is enough.

On the other hand, those who enjoyed the bliss of this visible bodily form find that they want to get human birth and serve Him or enjoy transcendental ecstasy. They pray for rebirth.

Life is an object having innumerable numbers and no origin or end like God. But God has been granting knowledge by offering the body (Thanu) sensory organs (Karana) as tools, the world (Bhuvanam) and experience (Bogam).

So, it has a resemblance to cosmic power.

It was immersed in the darkness of "ignorance."

It can be said that it is God's purpose to transform man into the highest civilized man by giving knowledge to him during every birth, just as the sun shines on the moon to enlighten him.

Even though man does not have all the highest qualities of God, as an extension of God, God gives man a body depending on his actions.

During the life of the giant complex chemical factory, the inborn desire-driven knowledge makes a decision that interferes with other lives' egos and causes harm.

This cause and effect results either in this life span or carried forward to future birth. The ego is enriched by the desires driven by inborn birth, or by information-based desires because there is no proper environment to regulate its desire, it repeatedly interferes with the freedom of other living beings and it multiplies evils.

Humans are always restless and brooding over worthless things having cravings and seeking innumerable demands originating from the mind.

Human beings are born with the idea that human beings can feel God's power very easily only through human birth.

Because of these sufferings through prayer, they get invisible knowledge of fore bearing the pain, and acceptance is born. So, sages are experiencing the given birth as good due to the grace of God and seek repeated birth.

The fragrance of the dawn was sweet.

The house is warm and the outside is cold.

The mind is an inanimate object.

That is why the body, the five senses, intellect, and ego (Sitham). Everything is energized by living beings. All of the body's tools are working as per signals emitted from life.

The mind does not know whether an act or object is sacred or not. It acts per the will of the intellect on one end and Ego, Sitham on another end all are delivering signals in accordance with the inborn desires.

You mean…

Sacred or not

Yes, if a thing is considered sacred it does mean that it commands respect from society through information-based knowledge constructed layer by layer, that touches the mind.

One has to find the sacredness of an act through knowledge.

God does not suffer from any kind of desires and dirt.

Lord is the remover of all kinds of dirt and crime.

If there is to be a process of elimination of guilt, there must be a desire for pleasure towards the Lord, which is the natural way of life.

Various places of worship, rites and rituals must have been produced by such men.

www.ingramcontent.com/pod-product-compliance
Lightning Source LLC
LaVergne TN
LVHW061622070526
838199LV00078B/7386